TODAY'S
SUPERSTARS

Eli Manning

By Mark Stewart

Gareth Stevens
Publishing

Please visit our web site at www.garethstevens.com.
For a free catalog describing Gareth Stevens Publishing's list of high-quality books,
call 1-800-542-2595 (USA) or 1-800-387-3178 (Canada).
Gareth Stevens Publishing's fax: 1-877-542-2596

Library of Congress Cataloging-in-Publication Data
Stewart, Mark, 1960–
    Eli Manning / by Mark Stewart.
       p. cm. — (Today's superstars)
    Includes bibliographical references and index.
    ISBN-10: 1-4339-1966-4   ISBN-13: 978-1-4339-1966-4 (lib. bdg.)
    ISBN-10: 1-4339-2159-6   ISBN-13: 978-1-4339-2159-9 (soft cover)
    1. Manning, Eli, 1981– —Juvenile literature. 2. Football players—United States—
Biography—Juvenile literature 3. Quarterbacks (Football)—United States—Biography—Juvenile
literature. I. Title.
    GV939.M2887S74   2010
    796.332092—dc22   [B]   2009008292

This edition first published in 2010 by
Gareth Stevens Publishing
A Weekly Reader® Company
1 Reader's Digest Road
Pleasantville, NY 10570-7000 USA

Copyright © 2010 by Gareth Stevens, Inc.

Executive Managing Editor: Lisa M. Herrington
Senior Designer: Keith Plechaty

Art Direction and Page Production: The Design Lab

Photo Credits: cover, title page Rich Kane/Icon SMI/Corbis; p. 4, 46 Larry W. Smith/epa/Corbis;
p. 7 AP Photo/David Duprey; p. 8 Andy Lyons/Getty Images; p. 9 Tannen Maury/epa/Corbis; p.
10 Lane Stewart/Sports Illustrated/Getty Images; p. 12 AP Photo/Reed Saxon; p. 13 Lane Stewart/
Sports Illustrated/Getty Images; p. 14 AP Photo/David Rae Morris; p. 15, 40 AP Photo/David Rae
Morris; p. 16 AP Photo/Dave Martin; p. 18 AP Photo/Ric Feld; p. 19 AP Photo; p. 20, 44 TRINACRIA
PHOTO/Shutterstock; p. 21 AP Photo/Bill Kostroun; p. 22 AP Photo/Bill Kostroun; p. 24 AP Photo/
Bill Kostroun; p. 25 Paul Spinelli/Getty Images; p. 26 Paul Spinelli/Getty Images; p. 27 AP Photo/
Tony Dejak; p. 28 AP Photo/Scott Audette; p. 30 G. Newman Lowrance/Getty Images; p. 31 Jamie
Squire/Getty Images; p. 32 AP Photo/M. Spencer Green; p. 33 AP Photo/Reed Saxon; p. 34, 41 AP
Photo/Marco Garcia; p. 36 AP Photo/Cheryl Gerber; p. 37 AP Photo/Disneyland, Paul Hiffmeyer; p.
38 Andresr/Shutterstock; p. 39 AP Photo/Julie Jacobson, file; p. 48 Matt Richman

Printed in the United States of America

1 2 3 4 5 6 7 8 9 14 13 12 11 10 09

Contents

Words in the glossary appear in **bold** type the first time
they are used in the text.

"What a play! David Tyree comes up with the ball! **WHAT A PLAY BY ELI MANNING!**"

—Sportscaster Marv Albert, during Super Bowl XLII

Eli Manning prepares to pass in Super Bowl XLII.

Chapter 1

Simply Super

Eli Manning scanned the field for an open teammate. The New York Giants were running out of time. They trailed the New England Patriots 14–10 in the fourth quarter of Super Bowl XLII. Manning dodged tacklers and twisted away from the Patriots as they clawed at his uniform.

Moments before Manning was tackled, he completed a long pass to David Tyree. When Manning rose to his feet, the football world saw a new superstar. It was an amazing pass under incredible pressure. "What a play! David Tyree comes up with the ball! What a play by Eli Manning!" sportscaster Marv Albert said. To Manning, however, nothing had changed. It was just another day and another play. There was a still a football game to win.

All About Eli

Name: Elisha Nelson Manning IV

Birth Date: January 3, 1981

Birthplace: New Orleans, Louisiana

College: University of Mississippi

Height: 6 feet 4 inches (193 centimeters)

Weight: 225 pounds (102 kilograms)

Number: 10

Family: Parents Archie and Olivia, brothers Cooper and Peyton, wife Abby

Not a Chance

The Giants weren't even supposed to be in Super Bowl XLII. Early in the 2007 season, many fans—and some of the team's coaches—did not believe that Eli Manning was ready to win the big game. Manning's teammates believed in him, though. As the Giants went through many ups and downs, the team grew stronger and more confident in their young leader.

The Giants won enough games to qualify for the **playoffs**. They would have to beat three excellent teams to reach the Super Bowl. Few believed they could. With Eli in charge, however, New York did just that.

Fact File

Manning led the Giants to 11 victories in a row on the road in 2007. One of those "away" games was in London, England. The Giants beat the Miami Dolphins.

Playing It Cool

The Giants beat the Tampa Bay Buccaneers, Dallas Cowboys, and Green Bay Packers. In each game, Manning showed that he was a championship quarterback. He stayed calm and cool. He waited for the defense to make mistakes and then took advantage.

Each playoff game was close. The Giants beat Tampa Bay 24–14 and Dallas 21–17. In the National Football Conference (NFC) Championship against Green Bay, the Giants controlled the ball for much of the game. The Giants won 23–20 in **overtime**. They were on their way to the Super Bowl!

TRUE OR FALSE?

More people watched Super Bowl XLII on television than any Super Bowl before it.

For answers, see page 46.

▼ Manning calmly directs a teammate with a Green Bay tackler chasing him.

7

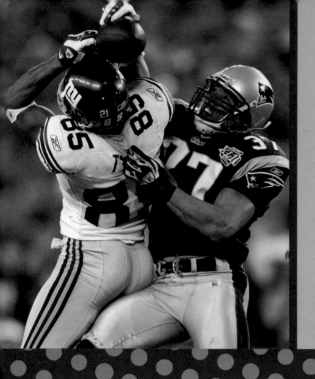

Fame Game

No one expected David Tyree to become a Super Bowl hero. He caught only four passes during the 2007 season. His catch late in Super Bowl XLII was one of the best ever. He pinned the ball against his helmet as he fell. If the ball had touched the grass, the catch would not have counted. Thanks to his moment of glory, Tyree made the cover of *Sports Illustrated* twice.

The Catch

The Patriots were unbeaten in 2007. They had won 18 games in a row. Still, the Giants were confident. They had nearly beaten New England at the end of the season. Eli Manning had to play his best.

And he did. In the fourth quarter, he threw a touchdown pass to David Tyree to give the Giants a 10–7 lead. The Patriots came right back. They scored and went ahead 14–10. The Giants had one last chance. They had to go 83 yards in less than three minutes. Manning's amazing pass to Tyree kept their **drive** alive.

Fact File

The Giants' victory in Super Bowl XLII meant a lot to New York sports fans. It was the city's first sports championship since the terror attacks of September 11, 2001.

Victory!

The Patriots kept up the pressure, however. They forced Manning to make another pinpoint pass with the game on the line. He connected with Steve Smith for a key **first down**.

On the next play, Manning saw clues that the Patriots were about to **blitz**. In a moment, almost all of the players would come crashing through the line. Manning took the snap. Then he quickly lofted a perfect spiral to Plaxico Burress for the winning touchdown.

TRUE OR FALSE?

Eli and his brother Peyton were the first brothers to win the Super Bowl's Most Valuable Player (MVP) trophy.

▼ Manning holds the Super Bowl trophy. Terry Bradshaw (left) interviews him and Coach Tom Coughlin.

"He truly just likes to play and **DOESN'T WORRY ABOUT ALL THE OTHER STUFF.**"

—Archie Manning, about his son Eli

Eli was born into a well-known football family. They are (left to right) Olivia, baby Eli, Archie, Cooper, and Peyton.

Chapter 2
Manning & Sons

Eli Manning was born on January 3, 1981, in New Orleans, Louisiana. The Mannings are sports royalty in New Orleans. Eli's parents, Archie and Olivia, are the king and queen. Archie was one of the best quarterbacks ever to come from the South. He was a star for the New Orleans Saints during the 1970s and 1980s.

The Mannings' football-playing sons were the young princes. Cooper (born in 1974) and Peyton (born in 1976) were older than Eli. They reminded people of their dad. They were fun loving and friendly. Eli was more like his mom. He was quiet and shy. Everyone knew the older boys would be football stars. But some wondered about Eli.

TRUE OR FALSE?

Eli's nickname in the Manning household was Eagle Eye.

The Big Easy

New Orleans is sometimes called the Big Easy. For Eli Manning, there was nothing easy about growing up as the youngest son in a football family. He knew that everyone expected him to be a football star one day. Archie and Olivia did not want Eli to feel this pressure. They did not force him to play. At home, Eli and Olivia smiled quietly while Archie, Peyton, and Cooper competed for attention.

▼ Eli poses with brother Peyton (right) and their dad, Archie (center).

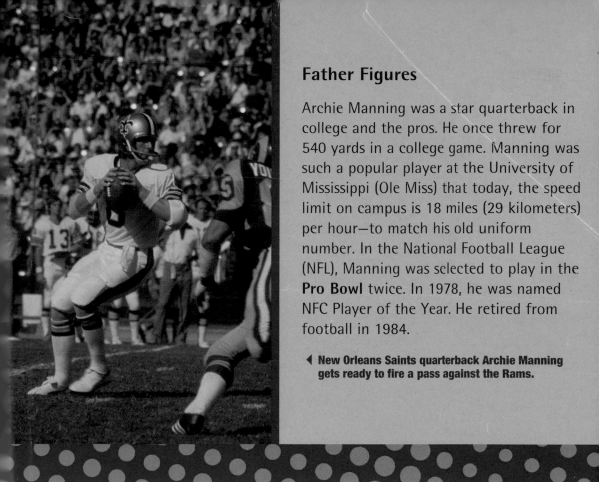

Father Figures

Archie Manning was a star quarterback in college and the pros. He once threw for 540 yards in a college game. Manning was such a popular player at the University of Mississippi (Ole Miss) that today, the speed limit on campus is 18 miles (29 kilometers) per hour—to match his old uniform number. In the National Football League (NFL), Manning was selected to play in the **Pro Bowl** twice. In 1978, he was named NFC Player of the Year. He retired from football in 1984.

◀ **New Orleans Saints quarterback Archie Manning gets ready to fire a pass against the Rams.**

Using His Head

Eli's brothers were huge football fans, especially Peyton. He would pin his little brother to the floor and not release him until he named every football team in the **Southeastern Conference**. This was not Eli's strength. "Eli's not big on sports history or statistics," his father laughs. "He truly just likes to play and doesn't worry about all the other stuff."

Eli had trouble learning to read as a child. Thanks to his mother's help, though, he quickly overcame his difficulty. He went on to become an excellent student.

Fact File

In honor of their
father, all three
Manning brothers
wore number 18
on their jerseys in
high school.

Passing Peyton

Eli Manning watched as his brothers
became the stars of the Isidore Newman
School football team. Peyton was the
quarterback, and Cooper was his favorite
receiver. Both earned college **scholarships**.

Eli joined the Newman High team
and also had great success. In his third
and fourth seasons as the team's starting
quarterback, Eli led the Greenies to the
state playoffs. Eli ended up breaking many
of Peyton's passing records.

Like Father, Like Son

Eli was a wanted man in his senior year at Newman. He received scholarship offers from more than 100 colleges in 1998. Archie and Cooper had gone to Ole Miss. Peyton had gone to the University of Tennessee. Where would Eli go?

The choice was simple. The head coach at Ole Miss was David Cutcliffe. He had been an assistant coach at Tennessee when Peyton was there. Cutcliffe had helped Peyton improve his game. So, Eli knew what he wanted to do. He picked Ole Miss.

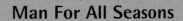

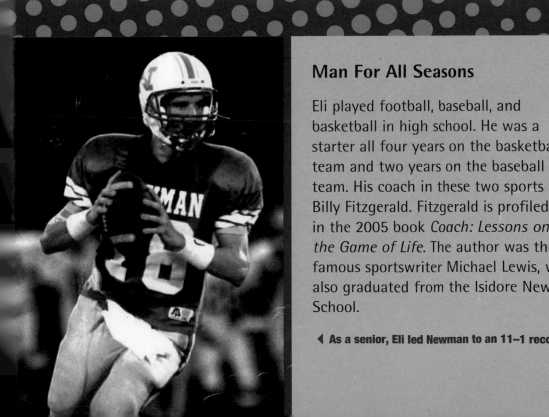

Man For All Seasons

Eli played football, baseball, and basketball in high school. He was a starter all four years on the basketball team and two years on the baseball team. His coach in these two sports was Billy Fitzgerald. Fitzgerald is profiled in the 2005 book *Coach: Lessons on the Game of Life*. The author was the famous sportswriter Michael Lewis, who also graduated from the Isidore Newman School.

◀ As a senior, Eli led Newman to an 11–1 record.

"I've never coached a player who has so much fun **JUST BEING OUT THERE PLAYING THE GAME.**"

—David Cutcliffe, Ole Miss coach, on Eli Manning

Eli Manning tries to fight off the University of Alabama defense.

Chapter 3
College Man

As a teenager, Eli Manning often imagined life as a college quarterback. He did not see himself standing on the sidelines during a game. Yet, in 1999 and 2000, Manning's job was to watch and learn from the older players. Coach Cutcliffe did not want to use Eli until the time was right.

That time came at the end of the 2000 season. The Ole Miss Rebels were losing badly in the Music City Bowl. Cutcliffe sent Manning into the game. He completed 12 passes and looked like the best player on the field. Ole Miss still lost, but when the 2001 season began, everyone knew who the starting quarterback would be. "I've never coached a player who has so much fun just being out there playing the game," Coach Cutcliffe would later say of Manning.

▼ Coach David Cutcliffe gives Manning advice during a 2002 game against the University of Georgia.

Passing Fancy

Eli Manning showed right away that he was a first-class quarterback. He gave Ole Miss a chance to win every game they played. Even in defeat, he was sensational. In 2001, he passed for six touchdowns in a 58–56 loss to Arkansas. Eli kept Ole Miss alive through seven overtimes!

Eli had a great year in 2002. He still had one year to go in college, but he was good enough to jump to the NFL. Ole Miss fans were overjoyed when he decided to stay for his senior season.

Heisman Hopefuls

The most important award in college football is the Heisman Trophy. The Heisman is given to the most outstanding player each year. In 2003, many fans believed that Eli Manning would win the award. He had a great year for Ole Miss. However, when the final votes were counted, Jason White and Larry Fitzgerald finished ahead of Manning, who came in third. Eli's father, Archie, also finished third in the Heisman Trophy voting, in 1970. In 1997, Peyton was the runner-up in the voting.

▲ The Heisman Trophy has been awarded to the best player in college football each year since 1935.

Golden Arm

In 2003, the Rebels traveled to the University of Florida. During their college days, Archie and Peyton had never won in "The Swamp." That was the nickname for the Florida stadium. Eli restored the family honor, and Ole Miss won 20–17.

The Rebels lost just one game the rest of the season. Eli was named 2003 Southeastern Conference Player of the Year. He also won the Johnny Unitas Golden Arm Award as the top senior quarterback in college football.

Fact File

Manning set or tied 47 school records during his four seasons at Ole Miss.

Brothers in Arms

Here is how Peyton and Eli compare as college quarterbacks:

	School	Years	Games	Completions	Yards	Touchdowns
Peyton	Tennessee	1994–1997	45	851	11,201	90
Eli	Ole Miss	2000–2003	43	829	10,119	81

TRUE OR FALSE?

The Mannings are the only family to produce three NFL first-round picks.

Draft Day

Every spring, all 32 teams in the NFL **draft**, or choose, the best college talent. In 2004, many believed that Eli Manning was the best quarterback available. That meant the team with the first draft pick — the San Diego Chargers — was likely to take him. The Chargers had the league's worst record in 2003.

Eli's father had been through this before. The Saints were a poor team when he joined them in 1971. No matter how well he played or how hard they tried, the Saints never got much better. Like any proud father, Archie wanted his son to play for a winner.

Super Swap

NFL teams often make trades on draft day. As soon as the Chargers chose Eli Manning, they began talking to the New York Giants about a deal. The Giants offered their pick—quarterback Philip Rivers—plus three other draft choices. The Chargers accepted, and Manning was thrilled. The trade was a good one—it gave both teams exactly what they needed.

Fact File

Eli Manning and Philip Rivers once worked as instructors at the same football camp.

▼ Eli Manning poses with coach Tom Coughlin after being traded to the Giants.

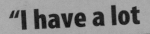

"I have a lot **OF WORK TO DO.**"

—Eli Manning, on learning the game as a rookie

Kurt Warner
(left) and Eli
Manning talk
football during
training camp.

Chapter 4
Pro Player

Eli Manning had everything a young NFL quarterback could ask for. He had a strong arm and quick mind. His new team, the Giants, had good running backs and receivers. But the **rookie** lacked experience. "I have a lot of work to do," he realized.

Until Manning was ready, the Giants' quarterback was Kurt Warner. Warner was a good teacher. He had led the St. Louis Rams to the Super Bowl twice. After leaving New York, he would lead the Arizona Cardinals to the big game in 2009.

Warner helped the Giants win early in the season. But he took a fierce pounding. His body began to break down. Before long, head coach Tom Coughlin had no choice—it was time for Manning to play.

Rookie in the Middle

The word *rookie* comes from the word *recruit*, which is what new soldiers are called. Eli Manning went from recruit to field general in his rookie year. It was quite a promotion. When he first joined the Giants in training camp, he looked unsure and nervous. He memorized all the plays in the **playbook**. But when it came time to make those plays, he felt like he was moving in slow motion.

Manning lost the first five games he started in 2004. In one game, he completed just four passes. Manning learned a little more each week. He finally won on the last week of the season.

◀ Manning changes a play at the line of scrimmage.

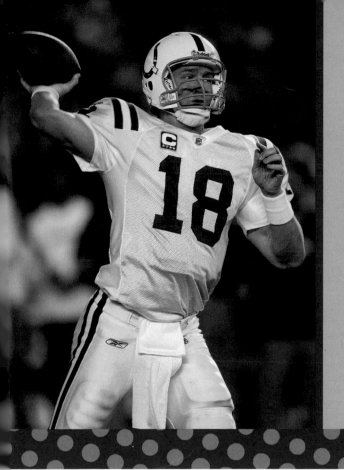

Yard Games

There are many ways to measure the skill of a quarterback. One way is to look at the number of passing yards he racks up during a season. In 2005, Eli finished the season with 3,762 passing yards. His brother Peyton had 3,747 (15 fewer) for the Indianapolis Colts. Peyton was still the better quarterback, but Eli finally had something he could tease his big brother about!

◀ Peyton Manning prepares to throw for a first down.

Getting It Right

In 2005 and 2006, Manning played great some weeks and poorly other weeks. This is typical for young NFL quarterbacks.

Manning knew his job was to learn from his mistakes. And he did. But when he played poorly, he often showed his disappointment. This tells teammates that a quarterback may lack confidence. In the NFL, this is dangerous. A team must believe in its leader.

Fact File

At the same time Eli played for the Giants, Peyton played for the Colts. When the teams met in a 2006 game, it was the first time in NFL history that brothers started at quarterback against each other.

▲ **Ben Roethlisberger throws a pass in Super Bowl XLIII.**

We Want Ben!

Eli Manning was one of three very good quarterbacks in the 2004 draft. Ben Roethlisberger and Philip Rivers were the others. Roethlisberger led the Steelers to the Super Bowl in his second year. Many Giants fans were angry that the team had drafted Manning instead of him. Of course, nine other teams had a chance to get Roethlisberger and passed over him, too. The Pittsburgh Steelers took him with the 11th selection in the draft. Picking quarterbacks is one of the trickiest jobs in the NFL. It is almost impossible to say how good a young passer will be in the future.

Be a Leader

After three seasons in New York, the fans were still not sure what kind of quarterback they had. After leading the Giants to an 11–5 record in 2005, Manning was terrible in the playoffs. He threw three **interceptions** against the Carolina Panthers. They beat the Giants 23–0.

In 2006, the Giants were struck by injuries. The team really needed Manning to take charge. When he did not, several teammates questioned his leadership.

Fact File

In 2005, Manning threw for 24 touchdowns. That was the most by a Giants quarterback since 1967. (Fran Tarkenton had 29 that year.)

The Proof Is in the Playoffs

During the 2006 season, the Giants' star running back Tiki Barber announced that it would be his last season. He wanted to go out a winner. In the final game of the regular season, he scored three times to give New York a victory. The Giants finished with an 8–8 record. That was enough to grab the last playoff spot.

The Giants faced the Philadelphia Eagles. Manning played great and gave the Giants the lead late in the fourth quarter. The Eagles came back to win, but Manning had proved himself in the playoffs.

TRUE OR FALSE?

When the Panthers beat the Giants 23–0, it was the first time since 1980 that a home team was held scoreless in a playoff game.

▼ Manning hands the ball off to running back Tiki Barber.

"With the game on the line, I WANT THE BALL IN MY HANDS."

—Eli Manning

Manning reacts to throwing a touchdown.

Chapter 5

Sensational Season

The Giants entered the 2007 season with questions. Who would replace Tiki Barber? Would their defensive star, Michael Strahan, play one more year? How would their best receivers, Plaxico Burress and Amani Toomer, deal with age and injuries?

The biggest questions were about Eli Manning. Fans wondered whether they would see the new Manning or the old Manning on Sundays. Barber was now a sportscaster. He told the world that he did not think Manning was ready to lead the Giants. These words stung the young quarterback. Barber had been a vocal leader. Manning felt that being a quiet leader was more his style.

TRUE OR FALSE?

Before the 2007 season, the Giants had won the Super Bowl four other times.

Ups and Downs

In the opening weeks of 2007, the Giants lost to the Cowboys and Packers. Manning injured his elbow and shoulder, and the season was in danger of slipping away.

Then the defense suddenly came to life. Strahan and Osi Umenyiora led New York's pass rush. The Giants scored victories over the Redskins and the Eagles. Then they won four more games in a row.

▼ **Michael Strahan celebrates after a tackle in 2007.**

By the Numbers

The Giants' offense relies mainly on running the ball. Even so, Manning's passing statistics from his first five seasons show he has the talent to get the job done.

Season	Completions	Yards	Touchdowns
2004	95	1,043	6
2005	294	3,762	24
2006	301	3,244	24
2007	297	3,336	23
2008	289	3,238	21

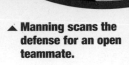

▲ Manning scans the defense for an open teammate.

Patriot Games

Manning played better after his injuries healed. His teammates were starting to trust him as well as believe in themselves.

The final game of the 2007 season matched the Giants and New England Patriots. The Patriots were 15–0. No team had ever gone 16–0 during the regular season. The Giants were determined to stop the Patriots—and they nearly did.

The Patriots pulled out a 38–35 win in the final moments. But it was also a "win" for the Giants. They knew they could compete with any team in the league— and beat any team in the playoffs. That included the Patriots in Super Bowl XLII.

Fact File

The season-ending game between the Giants and Patriots was shown live on CBS, NBC, and the NFL Network. It was the first time an NFL game was broadcast by three networks.

▲ Coach Coughlin praises Manning after a touchdown pass.

Road Warriors

For the Giants, the road to the Super Bowl went through Tampa Bay, Dallas, and Green Bay. Winning a playoff game on the road is very difficult. Winning three in a row is almost impossible. Manning played his best and led the Giants to three exciting victories.

Coach Tom Coughlin gave his players a plan to win each game. They carried out his orders to perfection. For Manning, the key was avoiding mistakes. Against the Buccaneers, Cowboys, and Packers, he did not throw a single interception.

TRUE OR FALSE?

Manning was just the second player to throw two go-ahead fourth quarter touchdown passes in a Super Bowl.

Super, Man!

In Super Bowl XLII, Manning led the Giants to two touchdowns, including the game-winner to Burress. He made the plays when they counted most. Afterward, Manning was named the game's MVP. Those who thought Manning was nervous in the final moments didn't know him very well. "With the game on the line," he likes to say, "I want the ball in my hands."

Fact File

Manning passed for 255 yards against the Patriots in Super Bowl XLII. More than 150 of those yards came when the Giants needed them most: in the fourth quarter.

True Value

Manning's Super Bowl MVP award put him in good company. Here's a list of quarterbacks who won the award in their first big game:

Player	Team	Super Bowl
Bart Starr	Packers	I
Joe Namath	Jets	III
Jim Plunkett	Raiders	XV
Joe Montana	49ers	XVI
Phil Simms	Giants	XXI
Doug Williams	Redskins	XXII
Troy Aikman	Cowboys	XXVII
Kurt Warner	Rams	XXXIV
Tom Brady	Patriots	XXXVI
Peyton Manning	Colts	XLI
Eli Manning	Giants	XLII

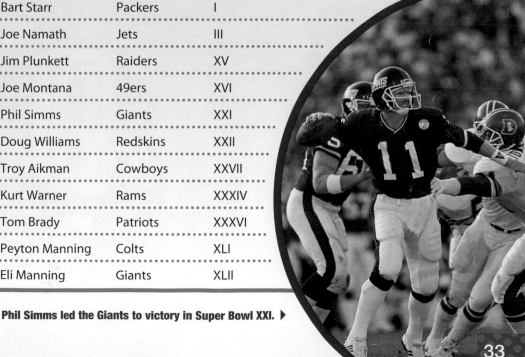

Phil Simms led the Giants to victory in Super Bowl XXI. ▶

"It's rare to have a best friend who is also your brother

AND ALSO AN NFL FOOTBALL PLAYER."

—Eli Manning

Peyton (left) and Eli Manning prepare to play in the 2009 Pro Bowl in Hawaii.

Chapter 6
Oh, Brother!

A year before Eli Manning won the Super Bowl, his brother Peyton had led the Indianapolis Colts to the championship. That made them the hottest "brother act" in sports. Before Eli's big game against the Patriots, Peyton was the brother who got a chance to have fun—and make money!— appearing in commercials and giving speeches. After the Super Bowl win, Eli was in demand, too. Besides, he jokes, "I think I'm better-looking than Peyton."

Of course, the person who demanded most of Eli's attention after the Super Bowl was his fiancée, Abby McGrew. They had met in college. Eli and Abby were married in April 2008, in Mexico. Peyton, his brother and best friend, was the best man.

▼ **Manning helps clean up the streets of New Orleans.**

Helping Hands

Archie and Olivia Manning taught their boys to help others in need. After their home city of New Orleans was flooded by Hurricane Katrina in 2005, Eli and Peyton were there to lend a hand. They helped purchase and deliver diapers, baby formula, and water to thousands of people.

While Eli was in college, he often visited patients at the University of Mississippi's hospital for children. In 2007, he began raising money for the hospital's Eli Manning Children's Clinic.

Manning About Town

Eli and Abby Manning are one of the New York area's most visible couples. They live across the river from Manhattan, in the New Jersey town of Hoboken. The people who knew Eli as a shy, quiet boy sometimes find this hard to believe. They never imagined he would feel so comfortable in a city where stars receive so much attention. "The standards for him are very high," says former Giants assistant coach Kevin Gilbride. "The city asks a lot of him."

Eli and Abby make large donations and attend events for many local charities. They also encourage others to get involved. Some of the hottest sports collectibles around are helmets and jerseys signed by Eli. He auctions them off to raise money for worthy causes.

▲ Eli and Abby Manning take a break at Disneyland.

Fact File

Abby was not a football fan when she met Eli. Would she watch football if it weren't for him? Eli says probably not!

Eli's Favorites

- ✔ **TV Show:** *The Office*
- ✔ **TV Reruns:** *Seinfeld*
- ✔ **Sport (other than football):** Golf
- ✔ **Music:** Country, Classic Rock
- ✔ **Fast Food:** Wendy's
- ✔ **Web site:** NFL.com

No "I" in Team

With a Super Bowl MVP in his trophy case, Eli Manning set out to do one of the hardest things in sports: win back-to-back championships. He had a good year in 2008, throwing 21 touchdown passes and only 10 interceptions. He also was named to the Pro Bowl for the first time.

Football is the ultimate team game. Manning played well in 2008, but injuries to other key players—including Burress and Tyree—hurt New York's offense. The Giants lost to the Eagles in the playoffs. Manning's dream of a second Super Bowl would have to wait.

Manning the Helm

Eli Manning may still have the shy, goofy smile of a teenager, but make no mistake—he is now a **veteran** quarterback. Even so, he still treats every game as a learning experience. Win or lose, he tries to find something that will make him better.

By keeping his cool, Manning has gained the trust and respect of his teammates. "He leads by example," says Tom Coughlin. "When he speaks, they listen." Indeed, Eli Manning has become a quiet leader.

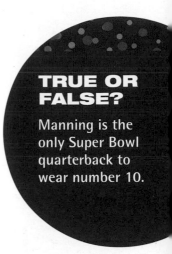

TRUE OR FALSE?

Manning is the only Super Bowl quarterback to wear number 10.

How Good, How Long?

How good will Eli Manning be? How long will he play? Unlike many NFL quarterbacks, Manning stands tall in the **pocket**. That means he trusts his blockers to surround and protect him. This gives him time to wait for teammates to get open. Many NFL quarterbacks like to throw on the run. They are exciting to watch, but often these players have short careers. When they lose some speed or are injured, they can no longer compete. As a "pocket passer," Manning should be around a long, long time.

◀ **Manning's career could be a long and exciting one.**

Time Line

1981   Elisha Nelson Manning IV is born on January 3, in New Orleans, Louisiana.

1984   Eli's father, Archie, retires from pro football.

1998   Eli breaks many high school passing records of his older brother, Peyton.

2003   Eli Manning is named Player of the Year in the Southeastern Conference.

2004   Manning is drafted by the San Diego Chargers and traded to the New York Giants.

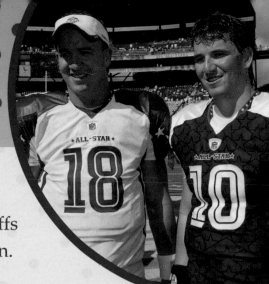

2005 Manning leads the Giants to the playoffs in his second season.

2007 Manning throws for 3,336 yards and 23 touchdowns. He leads New York to the playoffs for the third straight season.

2008 Manning is named MVP of Super Bowl XLII.*

2009 Eli and Peyton Manning play against each other in the Pro Bowl.

*The Super Bowl and Pro Bowl are listed under the year in which they were played. Both games take place in January or February but are part of the previous season. For example, Super Bowl XLII was played on February 3, 2008, but it was the championship of the 2007 NFL season.

Glossary

blitz: a defensive play that sends all but a few tacklers across the line of scrimmage

draft: to choose, the way professional teams select players for the new season

drive: a series of plays designed to reach the end zone

first down: a gain of a total of 10 or more yards that allows a football team to keep possession of the ball

interceptions: passes caught by defensive players

overtime: an extra period played when the score is tied after 60 minutes of regular play

playbook: a notebook that contains diagrams of the plays a team uses during games

playoffs: the games played after the regular season to determine which teams face each other in the Super Bowl

pocket: the area that blockers form around the quarterback when he drops back to pass

Pro Bowl: the NFL's annual all-star game

rookie: an athlete in his or her first season with a professional sports team

scholarships: money awarded to students who excel in academics or sports, to pay for their college education

Southeastern Conference: a group of college teams that play in the Southeast region of the United States

veteran: someone with a lot of experience

To Find Out More

Books

Horn, Geoffrey M. *Peyton Manning* (Today's Superstars). Milwaukee: Gareth Stevens, 2005.

Kelley, K. C. *Quarterbacks* (Game Day: Football). Pleasantville, NY: Gareth Stevens, 2009.

Stewart, Mark. *Football* (The Ultimate 10: Sports). Pleasantville, NY: Gareth Stevens, 2009.

Stewart, Mark. *The New York Giants* (Team Spirit). Chicago: Norwood House Press, 2007.

Web Sites

JockBio.com: Eli Manning
www.jockbio.com/Bios/EManning/Eli_bio.html
Find out biographical information, facts, and what others say about Manning.

NFL.com: Eli Manning
www.nfl.com/players/elimanning/profile?id=MAN473170
Here you'll find Manning's player profile, pro statistics, and more.

Pro-Footbal-Reference.com: Eli Manning
www.pro-football-reference.com/players/M/MannEl00.htm
This site contains Mannings's college and NFL statistics.

Championships and Awards

Southeastern College Player of the Year
2003

Johnny Unitas Golden Arm Award
2003

Maxwell Award*
2003

Heisman Trophy Finalist
2003

Cotton Bowl MVP**
2004

Super Bowl Champion
2008

Super Bowl MVP
2008

Pro Bowl Selection
2009

* An award given each year to the top college football player, as voted by coaches, sportscasters, sportswriters, and others.

** Although the game was played in 2004, officially it is the 2003 Cotton Bowl

Source Notes

p. 5   Marv Albert, Super Bowl XLII broadcast (2007), Westwood One radio network.

p. 13 Wendell Barnhouse, "Eli Manning follows the family tradition at Mississippi," *Knight Ridder/Tribune News Service*, August 29, 2002.

p. 17 Matt Hayes, "Easy Does It," *Sporting News*, September 30, 2002.

p. 23 WFAN (New York) radio interview, August 2004.

p. 33 "Eli Manning: Blurbs," TV.com, www.tv.com/eli-manning/person/284949/trivia.html.

p. 35 Lynn Zinser, "Eli Manning Has Teams Angling for Position," *New York Times*, February 22, 2004.

p. 37 Rick Gosselin, "NFL: A giant challenge awaits Eli Manning," WHAS 11 News, August 7, 2006, www.whas11.com/sharedcontent/sports/columnists/080806ccwcSportsColgosselin.1847b89.html.

p. 39 Jose Miguel Romero, "As the Giants QB, Eli is the Manning," *Seattle Times*, September 22, 2006.

True or False Answers

Page 7: True. More than 97 million people watched the game.

Page 9: True.

Page 12: False. His nickname was Easy, for his laid-back personality.

Page 20: True.

Page 27: True.

Page 30: False. Before the 2007 season, the Giants had won the Super Bowl twice.

Page 32: True.

Page 39: False. Fran Tarkenton wore number 10, but Eli is the first to win a Super Bowl wearing that number.

Eli Manning wears the number 10.

Index

About the Author

Mark Stewart has written more than 200 nonfiction books for schools and libraries, including histories on the Super Bowl and the New York Giants. He has authored biographies of Kurt Warner, Brett Favre, and Eli Manning's brother, Peyton—and worked with Dan Marino, Jim Kelly, Emmitt Smith, and 2009 Hall of Famer Randall McDaniel on their biographies. Mark has also written for Street & Smith's *Pro Football* magazine and *BLITZ* magazine.